BITES

SEVEN COURSES, ONE MEAL

Star Soup
Hog Roast
Cold Cuts
(Pickle)
Ice Cream
Jelly
And Hundreds and Thousands

First published in 2005 by Oberon Books Ltd
Electronic edition published in 2012

Oberon Books Ltd
521 Caledonian Road, London N7 9RH
Tel: 020 7607 3637 / Fax: 020 7607 3629
e-mail: info@oberonbooks.com
www.oberonbooks.com

A catalogue record for this book is available from the British Library.

Cover image: Stem Design

PB ISBN: 978-1-84002-536-1
E ISBN: 978-1-84943-868-1

eBook conversion by Replika Press PVT Ltd, India.

Characters

These are the hired help and they play all the parts.

CHEF
God-Magnate
God-Surgeon
God-General
Cop
Bus Driver
M Q
General

COOKIE POTTLEHEIMER
Sister 1
L
Lorraine May Fanoni

HARRY
Hakim
Sammy
B S

HARRY'S WIFE
Hakim's Wife
Phillip
X
P A
Sammy Jr

ANGELICA
Sister 2
V
Mo

Bites received its world premiere at The Bush Theatre on 14 January 2005.

Cast

Chef
Sister 3, God, Baby, Cop,
Bus Driver, MQ, General

Chris Jarman

Cookie Pottleheimer
Sister 1, L

Ishia Bennison

Harry
Hajji, Sammy, Boy Soldier

Owen Oakeshott

Harry's Wife
Hajji's wife, Phillip, X, Sammy Jr

Yvonne Gidden

Angelica
Sister 2, PA, V, Mo

Karina Fernandez

Director — **Lisa Goldman**

Designer — **Penny Challen**

Lighting Design — **Jenny Kagan**

Sound Design — **Sarah Weltman**

Mama Quillo would like to thank:
Everyone at The Bush, Jemima Lee and Sebastian Warrack at the Arts Council, James Hogan and Charles Glanville, Mel Stein and Team Sports Management Limited, Laurence Harbottle and The Peggy Ramsay Foundation, Carol Cooper and the Royal Victoria Hall Foundation, Martha Lane-Fox, Denise Powers, Margery Mason, Gillian Gane, Baroness Williams, Lady David, Liz Mansfield, Elisabeth Stuart, Hanya Chlala, Brian Voce, Mehmet Ergen, the Drill Hall, Rose Cobbe, Nathan Carr, Peter Carr, Simon Zagorski-Thomas and Afghanaid

Prologue

Moonlight.

A cold wind blows.

The 'diners' enter to sand – almost a lunar landscape, look again – mixed into the sand, decades of decomposing catering trash.

The hired help line up in welcome. They are all in uniform – filthy, torn, bloodied and bandaged.

COOKIE POTTLEHEIMER clasps hands and bows, HARRY leads them to their seats, HARRY'S WIFE pulls out chairs, ANGELICA offers 'menus', for this is the ruins of a diner.

From the detritus half-buried objects protrude, spoons and forks etc.

From a dark corner, CHEF watches, unsmiling, while sharpening two great knives.

Then when all the diners are seated – sound, a whirring…a stuttering jukebox … 'Catch…catch a…catcha'.

The hired help form a group. In close harmony they sing 'Catch a Falling Star', their voices fade. Perry Como takes over, a soft underscore.

COOKIE: Ladies and Gentlemen

ALL: Welcome
To our Banquet

HARRY: First course

HARRY'S WIFE: Soup

> *Lights dip. Perry Como fades then up to blinding light, scorching heat.*

Star Soup: Play 1

Three women – they stand and stare at the dust.

HAKIM'S WIFE: The well's dry

SISTER 1: Hakim's Wife
    spits
    on her child's
    lips

SISTER 2: And looks up
    to the hills

HAKIM'S WIFE: It's only
    four miles

SISTER 2: He's got the feet
    of a goat

SISTER 1: 'I'll be back
    in a jiff'

    She sniggers.

SISTER 2: Two days pass

    HAKIM enters, one foot is bandaged and bloody. He limps.
    He has water.

    They face each other.

HAKIM'S WIFE: You took
    your time

SISTER 1: She cannot
    say
    I love you

HAKIM: (*Apologetic, holding out water.*)
    I rescued
    a fly

SISTER 2: They boil
    Hakim's water

HAKIM gives the baby water.

HAKIM'S WIFE: No,
    a sip,
    let her sip
    you'll
    make her sick

SISTER 2: (*Whispering.*)
    The child
    wakes
    and sips
    and smiles

SISTER 1: (*Whispering.*)
    She has never
    seen
    this child

SISTER 2: Parvana

SISTER 1: her last child
    smile

HAKIM'S WIFE: (*Softly.*)
    It frightens me

SISTER 1: Hakim's foot swells

SISTER 2: He sweats

SISTER 1: Their days
    throb by

Tape of crying child.

HAKIM'S WIFE: I'll go up
    to the hills
    today

The women share a look.

HAKIM: They found a woman
in a cave
in her torn veil
a tiny babe

they dragged her
into daylight
tied her
to a post
stoned them to death

HAKIM'S WIFE: You know this?

HAKIM: Yes

HAKIM'S WIFE: You saw
her bones

HAKIM: I saw
the mess

He sits, his wife kneels and dusts his feet, she hands him a pair of cut and holey pumps and puts them on.

HAKIM'S WIFE: I like your feet

SISTER 2: She cannot
say
I love you

HAKIM'S WIFE: Most women
take to a face
with me
it's feet

HAKIM: (*Embarrassed.*)
Ssssh!

HAKIM'S WIFE: If
that foot

was
attached
to your neck
you'd
be reckoned
a
handsome
soul

HAKIM: (*Laughing.*)
You're mad

They look at each other. They are almost shy.

SISTER 1: She cannot
say
I love you

HAKIM'S WIFE: (*She whispers.*)
Don't get lost

HAKIM: Stay
out of sight

HAKIM'S WIFE: Don't get shot

He limps off.

SISTER 2: Hakim's Wife waits

SISTER 1 takes out a thick polythene bag full of dog biscuits and hands them to SISTER 2. SISTER 2 slams the bag of biscuits to the ground to make them break. They gather round like birds. Squatting, the two women take turns to knead the bag of biscuits.

Tape of crying child.

SISTER 1: If that child
doesn't eat today
she'll die

Do you hear me?

HAKIM'S WIFE: You've a big enough
gob on you

SISTER 2: You're looking
the wrong way

The women snigger.

SISTER 1: He won't
come back
the way
he went

SISTER 2: My man says
there are patrols
on all the roads

Tape of crying child.

SISTER 1: The desert dust
covers her

*The women are meticulously breaking the rock hard dog
biscuits into a powder. They are starving, not a grain must
be lost, they gossip in whispers.*

Did you hear?

SISTER 2: In the night

SISTER 1: Screams

SISTER 2: Samar

SISTER 1: Sharpening the blades
of two knives

You are my wife?
he whispered,
Yes, Jauma
And

I am your husband?
Yes!
I am so hungry
I must kill you wife
And eat you

HAKIM'S WIFE is laughing.

SISTER 2: Why are you laughing?

HAKIM'S WIFE: It's funny

Pause.

SISTER 1: If
he was going
to eat her
he should
have rested her;
six children
rushed
off her feet
dog biscuits
she's a stick
she'd be gristle
and bone

Pause. The two women size each other up.

HAKIM'S WIFE: (*To SISTER 1.*)
I say
we eat you

They snigger. SISTER 1 moves off in a huff.

Lights dip.

SISTER 2: It's night

She stands
under
the leering moon

HAKIM'S WIFE: Did you know
    that stars
    are born
    from dust?

SISTER 2: No

HAKIM'S WIFE: Oh yes,
    space dust
    and gas

SISTER 2: Never!

HAKIM'S WIFE: They're born
    in groups
    most
    break up

SISTER 2: Of course

HAKIM'S WIFE: You see
    that one

    She points.

    and that
    they're violent
    spinning balls

SISTER 2: You don't say

HAKIM'S WIFE: Hot
    and luminous

    forever burning

    the bigger
    the star

    the quicker
    it burns

    the shorter

and fiercer
its life,

some
are so massive
they explode,

It is
the
small stars

that

shine steady
and long

Hakim said

SISTER 2 moves away.

HAKIM appears. His feet are bleeding and bound. He walks painfully. HAKIM'S WIFE sees him. He moves forward, trembling she moves back.

He holds out the water.

HAKIM: It was boiled
    over a brush fire
    It tastes…
    sweet.

HAKIM'S WIFE: (*Almost inaudible.*)
    I thought
    they'd killed you

HAKIM: Poor little wife

    They're everywhere
    up there,
    they guard
    any lick of water
    If you don't have connections

they use you
for target practice

one shouts
'kneecap' they shoot
'bollocks'...bang
'heart
head'...bang bang

And they laugh
all of them roar
as your brains
split and splat

HAKIM'S WIFE: You can't go again
hear me
never again
this has to stop

We'll drink pee
for a day or two
then
we'll wait
for the next
army drop

Drink

HAKIM: No
I drank
up there

He hands water to her. She takes a slow sip. She is parched almost to death. A single tear might fall on her cheek. At last they touch tenderly. They sit side-by-side looking at the sky.

The stars
are so bright
in the hills

they make

rivers of light

I followed one

HAKIM'S WIFE: Yes?

HAKIM: Up

HAKIM'S WIFE: Up?

HAKIM: I tried to go down
I lost my footing
and the hillside
started to
slither and slide,
the night shivered
they shouted
I saw their torches,

I thought
best
take the path up
hide out
for the night;
In light
find my way back
to my nephew our friend

HAKIM'S WIFE: He wouldn't
let them kill you

HAKIM: So I climbed...

Higher
than I'd
been before

I came to a tree
hanging from it
hands and feet
like fruit
dripping

a bloody juice

Up higher
a rock
and stretched
across
a skin

of a
mad man
in one piece

drying
in the sun

eyeless
and
toothless

Still
as I passed
he grinned
and winked

Up higher to
a silver pool
of women's songs

Lullabies
songs to jig
at weddings
to hum
on the slow
death march

Hunger
sent me higher
to the very top

And there
under the clouds

I met God

GOD-MAGNATE: (*A Texan.*)
Hakim!

HAKIM looks astonished.

Great
you could
make it

Sit
Relax
Take the weight
off your…

He sees bloody bandages.

Now…

a few questions
you said

I was intrigued

His P A comes in with drinks on a tray.

(*Gruffly.*)
you took
your time

P A: I'm sorry
there was a problem
with the ice

There's a nice cool water
for Mr…

HAKIM: Hakim

HAKIM hesitates.

GOD-MAGNATE: Something
for the child

He takes out a packet of baby formula.

P A: I
picked it out
At the Mall

HAKIM takes it.

GOD-MAGNATE: For yourself

He takes out a pair of leather boots. HAKIM stares, incredulous.

P A: You don't have
to be a cowpoke
to step out in
Montanas

GOD-MAGNATE: But it helps

They both laugh.

P A: And for
the lady wife

GOD-MAGNATE: We'll keep
that up our sleeve,
the best
for last,
it's
good
people
practice,
a surprise
parting shot

He looks at his watch.

Now…?

HAKIM: Questions…

GOD-MAGNATE: Yes

HAKIM: Well,
 I'm a simple man

P A: We like that

HAKIM: Not educated
 but
 I've made it
 my business

P A: We like that

HAKIM: to find
 things out

GOD-MAGNATE: Go on

HAKIM: Well...

 He licks his dry lips nervously.

P A: Would
 you like
 a glass
 of water
 Mr
 Hakim?

HAKIM: (*Blurting it out, red faced.*)
 Why
 are there
 people
 who starve

 And people
 who
 have too much
 to eat?

 There...
 There...
 I said it!

A very long pause. GOD-MAGNATE and P A share a look.

GOD-MAGNATE turns to HAKIM.

GOD-MAGNATE: You'll need
to give me
a minute
on that one

He turns away and pretends to think. HAKIM and the P A are alone. She is embarrassed. HAKIM is shy. An awkward silence. She smiles easily, moves away fiddling with her clothes. HAKIM takes out one of the leather boots, inspects it, caresses it, smells it.

P A: (*Pleasantly.*)
He noticed
the holes in the soles
of your
sneakers

Try them on

HAKIM looks blank.

Your feet

HAKIM: No!

P A: Oh

Pause.

HAKIM: I'm thinking
maybe
I could boil
them

P A: Boil

HAKIM: Yes...
and...
and...

make a soup

P A: You'll make soup
from your boot,

that is so…
touching

Do you mind
if I jot
that down

He'll love that
We can
use that

Boot soup

That is…
catchy
Hakim

GOD-MAGNATE returns.

GOD-MAGNATE: You'll have
to come back
tomorrow

HAKIM: Tomorrow?

GOD-MAGNATE: For the answer,
or I can e-mail

HAKIM: No

GOD-MAGNATE: Oh!

Now
(*Looking at his watch.*)
if there's
nothing else

P A pleasantly tries to hurry him away.

HAKIM: There is something…
   (*Pause.*)
   A favour

GOD-MAGNATE: Anything

HAKIM: The hills are dangerous
   There are…brothers
   Who would take my life

   Could you
   make sure

   I get down
   safely
   to my children
   and my wife?

   Pause.

P A: We promise

   They fade away.

HAKIM'S WIFE: (*Tenderly.*)
   The thin
   mountain air
   squeezed
   your brain

   HAKIM yawns.

HAKIM: I almost forgot

   He roots about.

   He gave
   me a star
   to give you

HAKIM'S WIFE: A what?

HAKIM: A real star

from the Heavens

HAKIM'S WIFE: (*Smiling.*)
    Did he?
    A star
    Give it
    me
    tomorrow

HAKIM'S WIFE strokes his head.

HAKIM falls asleep.

She stands, takes up her watching position.

Long pause.

SISTER 2: Pssst

SISTER 1 wakes.

SISTER 1: What?

SISTER 2: Is she alive?

SISTER 1: I don't know

HAKIM'S WIFE: (*Very softly.*)
    I'm alive

The women creep forward. They whisper together.

SISTER 2: They found him

SISTER 1: Who?

SISTER 2: Hakim
    in the hills
    they shot him

SISTER 1: Dead?

SISTER 2: Yes,
    your son
    shot him dead

Pause.

But first
They cut off
his feet

Long pause.

SISTER 2: (*To HAKIM'S WIFE.*)
Did you hear?

HAKIM'S WIFE: Yes

Hakim is dead

Pause.

But first
he met God
who gave
me this

She holds out her fists. They are full of dust. She lets it trickle through her finger.

See
We can cook
Star Soup
See.

Juke box music: Jim Reeves, 'Home Cooking'. Lights dip.

ANGELICA steps severely out of her uniform. She wears bra, pants and peep toes. From the sand, she digs up a blackboard and chalk. She writes HOG ROAST.

Hog Roast: Play 2

GOD-SURGEON (played by the CHEF). He is removing bloody surgical mask and rubber gloves.

GOD-SURGEON: I take myself over to Al's Place every Thursday lunchtime. It's what we call 'a good ole boy' icehouse on JFK Boulevard corner of Voff St. I order a cold beer and a plate of Alvin's 'peel your own' shrimp, which he sprinkles with chilli salt, 3 parts sea salt, 1 part ground chilli flakes, a pinch of pepper, a spoon of brown sugar and a drizzle of his homebrewed peach syrup, I say brewed 'cos I know he puts a swallow of schnapps in it. Mmm mm they taste good, sweet and spunky.

Now it's not the sort of place my clients frequent, or my colleagues, but that's why I like it.

'Course, in the heat an' all, mosquitoes make a meal of you.

Thursday is Lingerie Day. This is a new thing. Lingerie Day means that for the customer's enjoyment a young female in her skimpies serves your shrimp.

Usually it's Angelica. She's a Mexican, with small high breasts and a kind of flat butt, wide but no meat behind, and slightly bow legs and she's that short and…stunted I've heard customers complain she may be 16…17, and I know she's 32 with six kids. She's pretty, mind; most of the women I have an intimate relationship with on the operating table, would give their firstborn for Angelica's skin.

I've only ever seen her in one outfit, black lacy bra and matching panties. For a small person she has surprisingly large feet, which she crams into what you ladies call peep toe shoes which I don't like seeing as how they make ladies feet look like hooves.

That day, that Thursday, I order a Shiner Bock and shrimp as usual; and Angelica serves, and as usual, she wears the same black bra and matching panties 'cept I notice the bow on the front of the lacy panties is starting to fray a mite, and she's sucking her pencil and she says

GOD-SURGEON / ANGELICA: (*Together.*) 'We ain't doing shrimp today.'

GOD-SURGEON: Angelica talks real quiet like with a papootie accent so you have to kind of lean in.

(*Together with ANGELICA.*) 'Cookie's done a hog roast seeing as how it's Alvin's birthday.'

ANGELICA: (*Together with GOD-SURGEON.*) 'She's told me to tell you she'd be honoured if you'd join them in the back yard.'

GOD-SURGEON: Cookie's Alvin's wife, and by rights, should be Lutheran but she sells raffle tickets for Life's Glory Mission that broadcasts on CNB with glamorous pastor Lorraine May Fanoni. And you'll know that little lady off the hoardings downtown…'best legs in the ministry'.

He chuckles.

Now, let's get this straight, you're talking 97 degrees in the shade and no one roasts hog in our state midday in August. But, I could see this whisper of hog smoke curling up to the blue sky and the perfume of that roasting flesh was making my mouth water, and Angelica turns and waves her paw at me to follow, which I was pleased to do seeing as how I got a real good view of her nakid butt through the lace panties which were fast disappearing up her crack.

Butts is my thing. Since the '95 court case I haven't done any face work, which isn't justice seeing as how Schlezinger cut through a woman's facial nerve so her eye kept winking on its own. But that was before the new legislation; anyway I'm stuck on butts, liposuction, stomach stapling and tucks.

They were all in the backyard, and sure enough in the heat of the day, they were roasting a whole hog over a log fire on one of those fancy turning spits 'cept they aren't really fancy no more seeing as how you can buy them flat pack at Kroger's; and he was a big fella, a 150 pounder with tufts of hair sprouting from his ears and a kind of embarrassed look on his face, and Cookie's bending over him, sweating, basting his back with a golden runny liquid off a big wooden spoon out of an aluminium bucket.

GOD-SURGEON / COOKIE: (*Together.*) 'Why sir you're just in time I was, this minute, about to carve.'

GOD-SURGEON: I didn't know anyone in Alvin's backyard. There was a couple of old ladies, several bare armed women in flowery frocks like Cookie, a whole brood of squeaky kids, in party masks, Wild Bill Hickcock and Geronimo. Alvin had a sprinkler going and folk took turns to stand under the fine mist to cool off. In the corner were four or five young cops, in uniform, strapped, but without their hats and drinking beers, and I saw one that looked like Al, only even bigger.

Alvin was sharpening two shiny knives and he introduced me as the Thursday Shrimp Guy, and everyone laughed and Alvin thumped me on the back and sliced me a giant cob of belly hog with a shard of crackling and the dripping fat made the fire sizzle and spit and smoke and Alvin gave me another ice cold Shiner Bock; and Cookie, still sweating, started carving and passing it around on paper plates, sticking the knife into the belly and larding the soft oozy fat on warm bread topping it with crispy crackling and a wedge of pink flesh. For five minutes no-one spoke, stuffing the honey hog into their pink, wet mouths, oohing and aahing, an old lady taking out her teeth to suck and slobber over the sweet hog chop, the kids' faces were shiny with hog fat, Alvin was snorting and making hog faces, chuckin' the ole boy under his chin, liftin' his soft lug and whispering sweet nothings and when he shoves his great index finger up the hog's ass and pulls it out and licks it and one small boy was laughing so much he choked and was dragged inside.

After about an hour, everybody stopped eating hog. Angelica was sitting inside in a dark, dusty, little corner pickin' on a wet lettuce leaf. Her cute little nose stuck in National Enquirer… 'Baby Alien Head found in Food Chain Pickle jar…'

Then the radio was turned up in the bar

Radio dance music. Honky tonk, ho down.

and a couple of the flowery ladies with vaccination marks up their arms, started dancing and Cookie was nodding in a rocking chair and Alvin put his finger over his mouth and took the wooden spoon dripping with the sweet golden liquid and started basting the top of the hot brick wall, where it spat and steamed.

GOD-SURGEON / COOKIE: (*Together.*) 'I know what you're up to Alvin Pottleheimer,'

GOD-SURGEON: Cookie says,

and Alvin Junior replies

'Come on Ma. It's Pa's birthday.'

After a minute a lizard about three inches long appeared

on top of the wall. It was still for a long time, the kids started to giggle, Alvin shushed, the li'l fella lowered his head and real dainty like started to lick the honey baste of the hot brick. Another came, and another, until there were… Jeez 15 or 20 and the kids started to get, a tiny bit, excited and then there were 20, 30 and I seen lizards but I never seen 40, 50 lizards in mid-town, in someone's back yard. One of the old ladies screamed; the first fella, full and sleepy, had dropped off the wall and was lying on it's back by her shoe, it's little claws scratching at the air and Alvin Junior suddenly grinned and turned to his dad and said,

'Are they a nuisance, Pa?'

and Alvin grinned

'They is a nuisance son, seeing as they upsetting the women folk'

and Cookie opens her eyes and says

GOD-SURGEON / COOKIE: (*Together.*) 'You be careful Alvin there's babies and old folks'

GOD-SURGEON: and Alvin and the young cops backed off and lined up and Young Alvin says 'best of five' and they popped at the little green lizards.

Bang!

Bang!

Bang!

And you couldn't see nothing 'cept a cloud of red dust from the brick wall and, when the dust cleared and they had stopped laughing, I saw green lizard splat all over the wall and here and there a little leg or a claw or a bit of lizard head and Cookie was a mite cross 'cept it was Alvin's 60th birthday and if a man can't have a lizard shoot in his own backyard with the full cooperation of the state law, when can he?

The ladies and the young 'uns had all gone inside only Angelica was there, still and quiet, and Alvin's son looked at her and said

'What you eyeballin'?'

in a hard voice so everyone stopped laughing

'Why you looking at me like I'm shit on your shoe?'

'Now son,' said Alvin 'cept he was unsteady on his feet and his eyes were blood shot.

'Looking at me like I'm shit on your shoe'

Someone laughed

'Fucking ho'

'Now son'

'Daddy pays you to put out squaw, and you're looking at me like I'm shit on your shoe'

'son'

'Wigglin' your skinny butt in front of decent family folk. Jeez, you think that respectful in front of old ladies'

'son'

'Wobblin' your saggy old tits in front of my baby cousins. Eh?

You lookin' at me like I'm shit on your shoe'

Alvin's son took the aluminium pot and hurled it at Angelica and it hit her on the side of her head and the golden liquid drizzled down her hair and face and the black lacy bra and that sure made me sore, Angelica being an acquaintance an' all and a quiet respectful kind of woman but she said nothing – nothing – and this riled Alvin Junior 'cos he screamed.

'You looking at me like I'm shit on your shoe!!'

and then he kind of jumped at her and he forced her to
bend over, pulling her down by her long black hair with
one hand and she struggled. I mean he is a seriously big
man and you've got to remember there's the whole of
62nd Precinct whoopin' him on and laughin' and you
can see me; and I've never been what you call good in
situations, and I mean this happened real quick, like
that (*He snaps his fingers.*) and she's bent over and she's
strugglin' an' cryin' an' I'm thinkin 'maybe I should say
something' and he kinda pulls the lace panties to one
side, then he shoves his index finger up her ass, he pulls
it out and then...and then...he licks it.

*Nirvana plays, lights dip. In moonlight, slowly ANGELICA
gets dressed. On the blackboard she crosses out HOG ROAST.
Nirvana fades.*

Cold Cuts: Play 3

SAMMY: (*Calling.*)
    Angelica

    Are you home?

ANGELICA: (*Gently.*)
    I'm home

SAMMY: Come up
    I'll rub
    your back

COOKIE: (*Whispering.*)
    His tenderness burns her

ANGELICA: In a moment
    sweetheart

COOKIE: His
    joints ache,
    sores
    weep
    some days
    he can't
    catch
    breath

ANGELICA: Go back
    to sleep

COOKIE: He thinks
    her love
    keeps death
    away

    Tape. Footsteps. A creaking door pushes open. In the room a TV is on.

ANGELICA offers SAMMY something.

SAMMY: What is it?

ANGELICA: Cold cuts

> Cookie
> had a hog roast
> for Alvin's birthday

SAMMY: (*Softly.*)
> Put it down

> Turn the TV off
> come
> into the moonlight!

Nirvana plays.

COOKIE: In the cracks
> in the ceiling
> she sees
> claws

SAMMY: Your breasts
> are so sweet

COOKIE: Hooked beaks
> tap
> at
> the broken pane

SAMMY: And your eyes…

ANGELICA: Their eyes
> glitter

SAMMY: Are so sad.

ANGELICA: Their great
> orange
> wings
> crash

through
the black glass

COOKIE: After
he sleeps,

Does he?

ANGELICA: Yes

COOKIE: After
the spell of her love

Is she pregnant?

ANGELICA: Yes

COOKIE: Her seventh child

Lights change.

Phillip
her first-born son
mended
the broken pane

ANGELICA: (*To a young PHILLIP, holding out a dollar.*)
Scotch tape
that's all,
you hear me?

No ice cream
No candy bar
No sparkly slide
for Mama's
pretty hair!

COOKIE: Her hand
strokes
his cheek

ANGELICA: Blonde hair,
blue eyes,

Phillip,
our American son

PHILLIP: I'll be back
in a jiff

COOKIE: How old is he
here
my dear?

ANGELICA: Ten, ten years old
the gentlest one

COOKIE: Tonight
time
see-saws

PHILLIP: When I'm grown up
I'll build you
a house
of our own

ANGELICA: Will you?

PHILLIP: I'll buy
you daisy
curtains

COOKIE: At the windows
yellowing sheets
of the
Trash Mags
shut out
stranger's
eyes

'Frozen sperm wife
gives birth
to dead Dad's
babe'

PHILLIP: And

a plump sofa
to sit on

ANGELICA sweeps the sand.

And a table
to eat
from

COOKIE: 'Flesh eating
   Bugs
   Make for
   Small town
   Horror'

PHILLIP: And shiny pots
   and…

COOKIE: 'Lizard man
   Sheds skin
   For
   Washington
   Sceptics'

COOKIE chuckles.

PHILLIP: …pretty plates
   And…

ANGELICA: (*Laughing.*)
   Where
   will you get
   all that money,
   Phillip?

PHILLIP: I'm clever
   I'll work
   we'll be rich

COP: (*Gently.*)
   Are you

Angelica Kline?

COOKIE: Six years on,
 a cop,
 with his hat off

COP: Is
 your husband
 at home
 Ma'am?

ANGELICA: Yes,
 but he's
 in bed
 my husband's
 sick

COOKIE: Tonight
 Time's
 a bullet

COP: (*Very gently.*)
 Do you have a son?

COOKIE: He notices
 her beauty

ANGELICA: I have
 three sons

COP: A youth,
 about 16
 a Phillip…Casey?

 Pause.

ANGELICA: Yes

COP: I'm afraid
 there's been
 an incident

 A shooting

In the
Montrose
area of town

COOKIE: Boys
go to
Montrose
to sell ass

ANGELICA: Montrose?
Well,
Phillip
never goes
to Montrose

COP: I'm sorry
to say

A body
of a boy

Has been
recovered
from a

derelict building

ANGELICA: A body!

I see
But,
what has this
to do
with Phillip?

Pause.

COP: I'm afraid
you're not
understanding me
Ma'am

Lights change.

COOKIE: In the
 City Morgue
 she strokes
 his cheek

SAMMY: (*Stricken.*)
 The boy
 was
 molly coddled.

 Tied
 to his
 mother's apron strings,

 Blubbering
 over his
 dead
 pet cat,

 Showers
 every day,

 fancy shirts,
 and shoes,
 and big ideas

 now see

 he's dead
 and
 a faggot!

 Just as well,

 At least
 a bullet's
 a man's death

 Unless
 it's up

the ass

He is sobbing.

ANGELICA: (*Very softly.*)
    What
    do you want
    to be buried in
    Phillip?

PHILLIP: Not buried
    Cremated!
    Out in a blaze!

ANGELICA: What
    do you want
    to be
    cremated
    in?

PHILLIP: The
    navy blue
    silk suit
    Mama
    and the
    Armani
    T-shirt,
    the
    Gucci
    shoes,

    Make sure
    the creases
    in the pants
    are sharp

    Oh!

    And play Nirvana

    Mama?

ANGELICA: Yes, Phillip

PHILLIP: I love you

Pause. A swell of Nirvana.

COOKIE: She leaves
    the cold cuts
    for
    her sleeping children

    Mattina
    who
    loves God

    Paulina
    who braids
    her hair
    with feathers

    Bradley
    who
    won't speak

    Inca
    with the
    brown skin.

    And Sammy Junior
    who
    makes her most afraid

    Who hums
    the Red, White and Blue
    while he pretends
    to shave

    Sammy
    who
    sets traps
    for Greys
    and wants

to be
a soldier

Tape.

*Footsteps…door creaks open. The night, car horns…shouts
and whistles.*

DRIVER: Where are you going?

The driver wears a hog mask.

COOKIE: Does the bus driver
have tufts of hair
out his ears?

ANGELICA: Montrose

COOKIE: The last bus
brings her
here
to these ruins
this desert;
to the
end of the world?

Lights change.

ANGELICA: (*Astonished.*)
Where's
the colonnaded mall?

Where's
the wall
of silver water?

Where are
the whitewashed
timber houses
with their front porches
swings
grandpas
and fat, pet cats?

The sidewalk cafes
and the gobble
of lives?

The twinkle lights
twisted
round palm trees?

The flashing neon signs

Eat all you can
At Seafood Sams!

Wilson's teeth brightener
For the whitest smile
in the state!

Vote Lee Brown
He's tough on crime

State Gun show
All comers welcome

SAMMY: Angelica…
    Angelica…

COOKIE: Back home
    her
    sick husband dreams
    of death

    Inside her
    So does
    the baby

    Lights change.

BABY: You can't
    go back

ANGELICA: No

BABY: So
    what

will you
tell him?

ANGELICA: I'll say
Cookie
had to lay
me off

I'll say
they took on
someone
younger

BABY: Prettier

ANGELICA: He hated
me working
there
anyway

BABY: You liked it

ANGELICA: No

BABY: Trolloping about
near naked

Letting
your titties
jiggle

Letting
your panties
disappear
up your
crack

Licking
your pencil

You enjoyed
their
hungry eyes

You
made them
drool

ANGELICA is finding it hard to breathe.

Who'll pay
the rent?

Mmm?

Don't
pay the
bills

You'll be back
in the queue
for bail bonds

ANGELICA is finding it hard to breathe.

And
how will we eat
without
Cookies'
Cold cuts?

Long pause.

Let's
get things
straight
now,
right
from the start

I won't
take
crap

Living
on a dung heap
with

the roaches,
sweltering
in the
stink

In the damp
dark
when the power's off

Cooking shite
out of tins
over fire

Stealing wood

Sent home
from school
for
smelling
swearing
scratching

Biting

Watching
the valiant veteran's
slow
soft
stinking
death

Listening
to the lies
in court

Listening
for the next
scream
from the skies

The next

rain
of ash

I simply
won't
have it

Do you
hear?

In the sand she finds a knife.

COOKIE: Rent boy's
    Ma
    Slits throat
    In
    Gay Sex den

Lights change.

SAMMY JR: Pa

COOKIE: Sammy Junior
    the boy soldier

SAMMY JR: I'm hungry

SAMMY: Here…

He hands him the plastic container.

SAMMY JR: (*He thinks.*)
    Is this
    dead animal?

SAMMY: Yes

SAMMY JR: (*He chuckles.*)
    It tastes good

Pickle: Play 4

LORRAINE MAY FANONI at her ministry. She is speaking into a microphone. Her sermon is in the style of the Second Baptist Church – fast, dramatic but 'homey' and from the heart.

LORRAINE MAY: (*Broad Texan.*)
Don't you
just love
the way

old folks

have of
hitting the
nail
on the head

My mama
God bless her
she's 85

and

knee high
to a gnat

and

she's
pickling
her own
home grown
vegetables

cutting up
cucumbers
and onions
and cauliflower

with this
real
shiny sharp
knife in her hand

and she says

'Lorraine May
I reckon
we,
that's us
American folks
I reckon
somehow
sometime
we got
ourselves
into a pickle'

Pause.

Sure
we're in a pickle
Mama

We've murdered
40 million
you heard me friends
40 million
helpless
mewing
American babes

And
God hears
I tell you friends
he hears the cries
when the iron
forceps
crush the baby

inside
the mama's uterus
and
the so-called doctor
removes
the tiny
broken bones
and tosses them
into black bags
like so much
trash
to be eaten
by dogs and
rats
disposed,
we are told,
in accordance
to state law

We're in a pickle,
cos
we're slaughtering
our own
future citizens
of the good old
US of A

While

opening
our loving
mothers arms
to
gun-toting
Aliens

Who bring
False Gods

Into our
kindergartens
our community centres,
supermarket queues,
our malls
our town councils
our Senate

And
I know
we're
in a pickle

When
I look
out my Dodge
and see
the crowds
of
young missys

on
the courthouse
steps

with their
ugly
placards

Begging mercy

for
a brutal
child killer
who tortured
a high school
prom queen

sweet little
blonde thing –

her folks
good people –
church going

You've seen
the photos

begging mercy
for her killer

cos

he's of
'subnormal
intelligence'

Sure he's of
'subnormal intelligence'

Do you think
a normal
God fearing
American boy
rapes
and kills?

I know
we're in a pickle
mama

when I switch
on
CNN

and I listen
to those

fancy suited
newsreader
hos

and their

smart arsed
lawyer type
dudes

mean mouthin'
our brave
boys and girls

in the military
overseas

risking
their lives
their precious lives
our children

For

Democracy!

Yes

Mama

sure we're
in a pickle

Pause.

What
do we do
to git out
the pickle?

Do we
cosy up
to the
big old
bad cauliflower
in there?

Or are we
the little

old
silverskin onion

sitting
on the jar bottom
underneath
the cinnamon stick
biding our
pickle time
hoping
nobody's gonna notice?

I tell you
what we do

We puff
ourselves up

And

We wriggle
a mite

till we're right
up the edge
of the jar
with the
fat old
gherkins
there

and then

we give
a mighty
push

and the jar
smashes
on
the pantry floor

and sure
there's glass
everywhere

and
the sticky
pickling vinegar

is
making
a reddish brown
stain
on our best
linoleum

and there's
cloves of garlic
peppercorns
big onions
baby gherkins

rolling about
all over
the floor

But you
know
what?

We're not
in a pickle

no more

and nobody's
gonna
eat us

Pause.

Anyone
who wants

a copy
of these teachings
for further study

might visit
my website
www.lifesglory.com

Thank you.

Ice Cream: Play 5

Pitch black.

Footsteps.

Pause.

V: (*A whisper.*)
Hallo…?

Hallo…?

Creeping footsteps. X pounces on her. They squeal.

X: (*Deep voice.*)
Gotcha!

V: Don't joke

Heavy footsteps. A third woman strikes a match. They look at each other, anxiously. Throughout they hardly raise their voices above a whisper.

L: Are we mad?

X: There's electricity

L: How?

X shrugs.

Have you checked
windows?

X: All boarded up
'cept for a small crack.
See
I hung a scarf.

V: (*In amazement.*)
We could
actually

turn on
the light?

L: (*Firmly.*)
No!

X: Anyway
it might be
better
in the dark

A sudden beam of sunlight, the scarf's come off its nail.

We see the fridge.

Panic, they bustle about fixing the scarf back on.

V: Oh, well done

L: Please
don't let's quarrel.

We see the ancient fridge. It has filthy fingermarks around the broken jagged handle. It looks as if it has been caught up in an explosion with blackened scorch marks from the ground up. Maybe it has bullet holes.

V: Does it work?

X: It's plugged in

V: Does it
keep things cold?

L: (*She touches it.*)
It feels cold

They lay hands on it. L opens the fridge. Light from the fridge illuminates the three women as in a Rembrandt painting. Inside the filthy fridge are several, hardly recognisable, items of food, growing fungus, and three small tubs of ice cream, newly placed.

They whisper.

X: Shut the door
   they'll melt.

   Door is slammed shut.

   Pause.

L: Look
   I have concerns.

X: No way

L: What?

X: I know
   what you're
   going to say.

   Was anyone
   followed here?

   They shake heads.

L: It's a risk!

V: I've waited
   weeks
   for this

X: I've waited
   years

   *X takes out a well-licked spoon and stands at the ready. V
   takes up her spoon.*

V: What will
   it taste
   like?

X: Mountaintops

V: What will
   it smell
   like?

X: Mothers

V: What will
   it feel
   like?

X: A lover

L: You mustn't
   say that
   to her

X: Of course I must say that

   What's
   the matter
   with you?

L: Don't shout

X: Open the door!

   *L opens the door and hands out the out the tubs as if offering
   communion.*

   Now,
   it's
   V's first time

   Looks at V. V takes off the lid, she looks at it.

X: Lick it

   She does so, she smiles, she takes off the paper, she looks at it.

X: Lick it

   She does so, she smiles.

V: Oh, look,
   it's in
   two perfect
   halves

   They all peer.

X: Vanilla

V: (*In awe.*)
Vanilla

X: And chocolate

V: (*A whisper.*)
Chocolate

V tries to decide which to taste first, her spoon hovers. X snatches it and scoops out half and half and she feeds it to V. V's expression changes.

(*Softly.*)
Mountaintops
and mothers
and...
and...

Oh
I don't think
I can bear it

They compose themselves, they are about to take off the lid.

X: Hang on

From her clothing she takes out a red lipstick and a small mirror. Meticulously she paints her lips.

Now

X and V giggle nervously. Synchronised they each take off the lid and then the paper, they lick it. Then, slowly, sensuously, they spoon up the ice cream. L's spoon hovers. She cannot eat.

X: Tell you what.
I'd like
to cover my old man
in this stuff
and slowly lick it off.

V: Oh, oh.
   It's hard
   in the mouth
   and then
   soft

X: She's
   learning fast.

   X and V giggle, suppressed hysteria.

   I last
   ate ice cream
   in Kabul
   market place
   in 1969

   I was 13
   A pink dollop
   In a crispy cone

   We shared it.

L: (*Surprised.*)
   Did we?

X: Yes,
   Why
   can't you remember?

V: You're lucky to have memories.

X: This
   is a memory
   now

   Coming out,
   coming here
   meeting us
   and
   eating ice cream.

V: Thank you.

L: Don't thank me,
   don't anyone
   thank me.

X: (*To V.*)
   One day
   You will
   share
   a dainty
   silver spoon
   of ice cream
   on a
   sunny shore
   with
   a dark-haired
   dimpled boy

   One day
   I will eat
   ice cream
   in Kabul
   market place
   again
   with my old
   friend.

   You ordered
   me to give
   my little one
   ice cream
   every night
   when he was
   ill.
   Remember?
   Years ago.

L: Did I?

X: Yes,
    you did.

   Pause.

   One day
   you'll be a
   doctor
   again

   *Without warning the electric light is switched on. Startled,
   the three women blink and face front.*

   Blackout.

   Lights up.

   *A large, hairy man, M Q, sits on top of the fridge. L has been
   made to kneel. An eleven-year-old boy soldier is cleaning a
   huge rifle. He is guarding.*

B S: They
     have been taken
     to
     The Department
     for Promotion
     of Virtue
     and
     Prevention of Vice

M Q: (*Softly spoken.*)
     What
     a mouthful
     from the boy,
     I prefer
     Department
     of
     Religious Observances

L: What
   will happen
   to them?

M Q: You
    may tell her.

The boy laughs.

You frighten
the lady
be more
respectful.

They'll be questioned.

L: They
    have done nothing
    to attract
    the attentions
    of your
    Department

M Q: The eating
    of ice cream
    in a public place
    by women
    is forbidden.

L: But
    this is not
    a public place.

M Q: It is
    a teashop.

L: A burned out
    teashop.
    A ruin.
    It is
    my uncle's
    closed-up
    ruined teashop

    Therefore
    it is

a
private place.

M Q: (*He smiles.*)
And
one of your
friends
was wearing
lipstick.

The boy makes lewd noises.

You see
what the
wearing
of lipstick
does to this
young boy!

L: I will
give
evidence
in any court of law.
Her lips
are
not painted
but
a natural
deep
red hue.

B S: Her shoes
went
click, click, click.

M Q: Women
must refrain
from hitting
their shoes
on the stones

to make sounds

B S: Because
    it
    inflames me!

    M Q laughs.

L: And
    why am I
    here?

    Long pause.

M Q: Long ago
    I was
    your patient

    L looks up.

B S: Lower your eyes
    whore.

    She looks down.

M Q: (*Softly.*)
    Do you
    remember
    me?

    Pause.

L: I remember
    nothing

    From outside, in the near distance, the sound of bombing.

M Q: Excuse me
    Watch her.
    Don't
    hurt her.

    He goes. Silence.

L: What's that?

B S: They're bombing
us
I reckon.

L: God help us.

The boy is cleaning his rifle. He traps his finger.

B S: Ow!

He sucks his finger.

L: Let me
see it.

He shows it to her.

B S: It's made a blood blister.
I've dozens,
see,
it always
happens.

L: You must be more careful.

Pause.

How old
are you?

B S: Eleven

but
I've seen life
I tell you
out
on the streets
out
on patrol

with
my whip

and my
big
state issue
stick.

If
I see
a woman
acting
without dignity
decorum
or
due respect

I lash
her ankles
such.

He shows and laughs.

They flinch
and hop.
I leave
them
pretty
anklets
of blood.

Outside, gunfire, a couple of shots.

I've never
shot
a woman.

L: (*Sorrowfully.*)
   Only eleven,
   you are
   big for your age.

B S: (*Leaning forward, lascivious.*)
   Whore!

I'm spoken for
I've a…wife.

L: Where's
   your mother
   your family?

B S: I don't
   have a mother,

   never had one.

   My mother
   is
   The Holy State

   My father
   is
   The Holy War

   The soldiers
   are
   my family.

   They raised me.
   (*Proudly.*)
   At eight
   I loaded
   Artillery.

   At nine
   lugged
   ammo.

   At ten
   guarded
   installations.

   Now,
   I am eleven
   and a soldier.

Is there
ice cream
in there?

L: Open it

He does so, he takes out the tub of ice cream, he looks at it, smells it.

B S: I've never had ice cream
never
in my life.

L: Have it.

B S: NO!!
It's forbidden.

Pause. Carefully, fearfully he puts it back.

L: What
will happen
to my friends?

B S: The old one
will be
shot.

L: For eating
ice cream?

B S: For whoring.

L: I will swear
in any court of law
my old friend
has never
prostituted herself.
Never.
I will swear.

B S: As
　　for the
　　girl…

　　She wasn't touched
　　I reckon.
　　You can't
　　execute
　　a virgin.

　　They'll do
　　the two finger
　　test.

　　If it's true

　　They'll take
　　her
　　round the back
　　to…

　　…have some fun.

　　Then execute her

　　He laughs. L starts to gasp for breath.

　　Don't worry
　　you'll be all right.
　　He likes you

　　M Q enters. He appears very agitated.

　　They're bombing us.

M Q: Yes.

B S: (*To L.*)
　　You won't
　　have to worry
　　now
　　about your friends

they'll target
the Department.

He makes aeroplane-bombing noises.

L: (*To M Q.*)
Please...
tell me.
What
will happen
to my friends?

M Q: It's lucky
I was
on the spot,
bombing or not

They'll
be shot

in the
stadium

next Friday.

Beware

We'll
make examples.

No one
is above
the
Holy Law

Not
enemies
or
friends

L looks up in astonishment.

L: (*Soft and incredulous.*)
   I remember.

B S: Lower
   your eyes
   whore!

L: I remember…
   I remember
   You.

   A boy,
   gentle
   and so
   devout

   he made
   us smile.

   You lost
   a leg

   The men
   had tried
   to cauterise
   the wound.

   But you
   got gangrene.
   I remember
   you screamed
   when we
   cut
   the bandages.

   The shock
   made you
   bite through
   your tongue.

I nursed you
for weeks
no, months.

I cleaned
up
your pee
your shit
your sick.
I wiped
your nose.
I combed
your soft hair.
I washed you.

I brought
my own sons'
shirts

and shoes.
I remember
I taught
you
to speak
again.

And
every night

I held you
crying
for your
dead mother.

Your fists
tight
with anger

Your eyes
Red

and swollen.
I remember you
sobbing
into the pillow
inconsolable.

'Mama,' you
cried
'Mama
My Mama
Mama'

I remember
I remember.

A dreadfully long silence. B S looks at M Q. M Q is shaken.
B S lets out a snigger.

M Q: Go to the fridge
will you, boy?

B S goes.

What do
you see?

B S: I see
a tub
of ice cream.

M Q: Would
you like
to try
this
ice cream?

B S: I would
like it
very much.

M Q: If you shoot

this woman
I will give you
the tub
of ice cream.

B S gets his rifle points it at L's head.

B S: My first time.

Blackout.

One shot.

Jelly: Play 6

Bright lights – two young men.

MO: Dad built a hutch for my rabbit, in the backyard…
Kevin, he was called - the rabbit, not my dad – out of
chicken wire and an old kitchen cabinet…banging and
hammering away, all through Saturday…Brookside,
Barrymore…

Of course, Mam went ballistic…

Anyway, right little palace it turned out in the end –
curtains up at the window, pebbles round the door, Dad
even landscaped a dandelion patch garden. What do
you think of that?

Pause.

Yes…yes, indeed…indeedy…he was one very happy
bunny.

Slight pause.

My dad, not…Kevin, no…next door's mutt ate the
rabbit.

Pause.

To SAMMY.

You have any pets?

SAMMY JR: Mmm?

MO: When you were a kid?

SAMMY JR: No, no pets. (*He thinks.*) My pa had a gecko
he kept in a cage in his bedroom.

MO: Don't tell me, he called it Shania. No? Gordon? …
Frisky?

SAMMY JR: I…don't remember.

Pause.

MO: It wasn't wasted, the rabbit hutch. My sister kept her Barbies in it, the old ones. She'd take them down to the backyard, put talc in their hair, some of them, they were the wrinklies; others, she'd cut the legs off, they were the children; draw beards and moustaches with felt tips, they became the blokes. She made families; grandmas, aunts, uncles, cousins and she and her friends would play for hours. I used to listen from the entry… (*He acts out 'dolls' with his hands, he is in shackles.*) 'Come on Daddy, let's take our baby to Tesco's…bad baby…bad baby, being sick over Grandpa.' Weird…I mean, so weird!

Do you think she still does all that?

Pause.

SAMMY JR: How old is she?

Pause.

MO: Thirteen, now, fuck… Remind me to ask her, will you, next time I write?

Pause.

Do my letters get sent?

Pause.

SAMMY JR: Not all of them.

MO: Appreciate your honesty… No, really, I appreciate it. What's your name again? Hank did tell me.

SAMMY JR: Sammy.

The sound of building work, banging and hammering which continues intermittently through the scene.

Pause.

MO: He's not coming back then?

SAMMY JR: Who?

MO: Hank, of course

SAMMY JR: No.

MO: Never ?

SAMMY JR: Never.

Pause.

MO: And you're from Texas.

SAMMY JR: That's right.

MO: Like Hank?

SAMMY JR: Yes

MO: (*Phoney Texas accent.*) Born and raised in Texas Sugarland, same as my pa and his pa before him.

SAMMY JR looks at him. MO laughs, taps his nose.

SAMMY JR puts his paper down and looks at his watch. He picks up a clipboard.

SAMMY JR: (*Reading from clipboard.*) In November 2001 –

MO: Here we go –

SAMMY JR: – in a cave in Eastern Afghanistan –

MO: (*Singing, as football chant.*) Here we go…here we go… here we go…

SAMMY JR / MO: Near the city of Gardez

SAMMY JR: a substantial amount of gelignite napalm was found.

MO: But, and correct me if I'm wrong you're mixed blood, Sammy, old man?

SAMMY JR: Were you aware of the existence of this cave?

MO: Sugar and sp…Spanish…? No! Something further back – Mexican! No problemo. Me, I love mixtures!

He mimics a huge explosion.

We had this right nutter at school…Mr Spink… chemistry teacher – I loved chemistry, my favourite subject – he had a thing, Spink, for mixing things up, explosions, the old acetylene and air trick… Singed his fringe every science week for yonks, the prat.

Spare a ciggie, old son?

SAMMY JR throws him one.

(*Surprised.*) Cheers, mate, nice one.

Pause.

He was a bit of a randy git, Spink, had this rusty old Jag with leopard print seat covers. He'd pick up Miss Reims every Wednesday afternoon, after trampoline club, take her to the waste ground opposite Our Lady of Victories for a bit of trampolining of his own. She had a face like a well-trodden hockey pitch but bazookas to die for, big and bouncy like netball balls, my favourite they are.

Pause.

You got a girlfriend, Sam?

SAMMY JR: Yeah, yeah, I got a girl.

MO: You surprise me, 'cos we all thought…

Pause.

(*He smiles.*) We all thought…

SAMMY JR: Yeah…?

MO: Forget it. Forget it right, barking up the wrong 'un old son, muchos apoligoses. You're like me then?

SAMMY says nothing.

I hate faggots me, if it was up to me, I'd put every fucking faggot against a wall and use his bollocks for target practice.

He mimes a gun.

Pow! Pow! Pow! What do you say old son?

SAMMY says nothing.

Do you know – and I haven't told anyone this, not Hank, not anybody. I haven't had a stiffy, not a proper one, since I've been in here. Wonder if I'll ever have one again.

The hammering gets louder. They share a look. MO laughs.

Not enjoying yourself in here, are you Sam?

SAMMY JR: Enjoying myself?

MO: Don't be shy, perhaps I can help, Hank and I used to have some lovely chats, you know – man to man. Yes, indeed, quite a conversationalist, our Hank.

SAMMY JR: (*Suddenly edgy.*) I never listened to his crap.

MO: It's getting to you right…being in here. Well it would wouldn't it, you realise of course, that they know.

Pause.

SAMMY JR: Know?

MO: Sarge thinks you've got no fight in you, Hank said no fizz, no fist, he'd like a bit more spite…

Leg out to trip, ball of the foot rammed against the back of the neck.

It was noted that when they cut down whistling Ali, and it was a messy business, I agree, you 'averted your eyes'.

That's what I heard, you blink too much.

SAMMY JR: Blink?

MO: Lick your lips, bite your nails, they've opened a file 'Private Samuel Kline Junior averted his eyes and was not able to be useful in the following moments.'

SAMMY JR: Useful?

MO: Now Hank, was very useful. He actually enjoyed India block, that's where I met him, kneeling, blindfolded, hands and feet shackled. Me, that is, not… Hank. 'Course there's no windows, the roof's tin, one light bulb dangles, he turned the air conditioning up so it's brass monkeys and took the blanket, following strict orders from the General, of course, well, when he opened the door next morning. I was shaking (*He demonstrates, comically.*) …couldn't stop friggin' shaking. I'll say this for Hank, he liked to laugh.

SAM takes up the clipboard, his hands shake.

Here we go.

SAMMY JR: In November 2001.

MO: If you want to know where Osama is last I heard he was working on the door at 'The Sands' Cheetham Hill.

SAMMY JR: In November 2001, a substantial amount of gelignite napalm was found…

MO: You've put in for a return to active…haven't you, Sammy? Hank spilling the beans again.

You wouldn't get me going back there, no fucking way. Saw some nasty sights, Sam. Well, so did you I'm sure, things I couldn't repeat…wouldn't…bits of kids with their dicks cut off, rolled bank notes shoved up their noses, a pile of dead women under a cloud of flies, like a pile of red rags, their throats slit…their throats slit…

Pause.

Just like your Mam, eh, Sam?

Pause.

Just like your old lady…

Pause.

SAMMY JR is breathing deeply, he is turning red and sweating.

Suddenly and with astonishing viciousness, he knees MO in the groin. MO recoils, he is in agony, whimpering. SAMMY JR goes to a corner.

Nice one, Sam. You did Sarge proud.

Long pause.

Both men are squatting, head in hands, strange noises are coming from SAMMY JR…he is trying to stifle his sobs.

(*Softly.*) Pull yourself together, you fucking… You fucking saddo…they're looking at you see, they're all looking at you, you sicko. You're finished mate. I'm telling you, you're finished in here…you sick saddo

Pause.

SAMMY JR stops sobbing.

SAMMY JR: They couldn't get him down

MO: I don't need to hear this

SAMMY JR: (*Laughing.*) They had to radio for scissors.

MO: Shut it, right? …fuckin'…

SAMMY JR: His face was turning…black. He was still trying to…

MO: – pray, that's what I heard –

SAMMY JR: His whole body was…twitching. There was a sweet smell…he'd shat himself…

MO: He was frightened…he wasn't sure how to do the knot.

SAMMY JR: And he was old, you know, an old man, a silly old fool he was, course he couldn't speak English…

MO: He gibbered.

SAMMY JR: If ever you touched him, he was icy cold, and clammy, always.

MO: When they pushed him off the plane, he broke his nose, he whistled every time he took a breath…

SAMMY JR: Yes

SAMMY JR continues to snivel. MO watches, then paces… He looks out, as if to call for help.

SAMMY JR stands, he takes deep breaths, he wipes his eyes.

I'm sorry.

MO looks at him.

MO: Did he…?

SAMMY JR: Live? Yes. Unfortunately.

Pause.

MO: I wouldn't worry too much, he'd been hanging there for ages…not much you could have done, and… p'raps he was a nice old bloke, I don't know, but he seemed a bit of a, you know, head case before, actually…you know, a bit of a loony and I reckon he'd probably done some really bad things in his time, I mean, I can't swear but I'd say probably…by the look of him

SAMMY JR: And he stank

MO: Like a sewer

SAMMY JR: And he picked his nose

MO: His feet

SAMMY JR / MO: (*Together.*) His arse

They both laugh.

Pause.

MO: Your friend, Hank liked us all to talk dirty to him.

SAMMY JR: Yes.

MO: It earned the odd extra fag…sandwich, sometimes…
but he always made a beeline for whistling Ali, I don't
know why. P'raps he fancied him.

They both laugh.

I'd have definitely put him down as a screamer

They laugh.

SAMMY JR: I mean, he did have tits.

More laughter.

The sound of banging and hammering.

MO: I thought they'd finished the court rooms.

SAMMY JR: They have

MO: I see, so what's this then?

SAMMY JR says nothing.

Fucking hell, I should get a real stonker on with 20,000
volt up me

Pause.

SAMMY JR gets his clipboard.

I don't mind dying actually. It's just my mam'll be upset

SAMMY JR: In November 2001, a substantial amount of gelignite napalm and other explosive gelatinous substances were found in Eastern Afghanistan, near the city of Gardez, known to be occupied as part of the stronghold of the resistance to the allied forces. Were you aware of the existence of the cave?

MO: We made a firework once in chemistry with Spink

SAMMY JR: Were you ever there?

MO: A rocket. It should have been holiday revision, but no girls turned up and Spink was bored.

75 per cent saltpetre, 15 per cent charcoal and 10 per cent sulphur makes black powder, if you want a boom, mix perchlorate, Sammy. But that dark night Spink wanted stars! Magnesium or aluminate makes white stars, sodium salt makes yellow, carbonate for red, barium nitrate for green, copper salt for blue.

Now an unlit star isn't much to look at, a black lump, size of a nice bit of block.

Stars are…contained in separate containers, see, each with its own bursting charge and I tell you the more the compartment can resist this bursting the more… fantastic…fantastic the display!

Lights dim.

It was teatime, winter, the nights had drawn in. Spink took us onto the playing field. It was black and freezing. No moon but icy stars and the grass was crunchy.

We climbed past the new sports pavilion to the highest ground to a sort of grassy mound; an old burial mound they reckoned, old souls. Spink planted the rocket at the very top, we backed off.

He lit the touch paper with his lighter and then scarpered. First it fizzled, we thought it had gone out. Spink was about to try and relight when suddenly, unexpectedly, with a splutter of tiny sparks and with an almighty bang, it whooshed high into the sky, making a perfect arc of yellow light, an arc of yellow stars.

Pause.

The world seemed quieter after our great bang and even darker.

'Well, fuck me,' said Spink and giggled. He tried to light a ciggie but his hands shook. He took out his silver hip flask and passed it round. We all took a sip and I thought, 'Mam'll kill me.'

It was our rocket, Spink and 5B Bosley Heath. We had made stars that night and we were not just men but Gods!

Determined.

Yes.

Long pause, then, suddenly.

Go home, Sammy, eh? To Sugarland. Why don't you just go home?

SAMMY JR: (*Softly.*) Yes, yes, I will...one day.

Slight pause.

MO: Do you miss her?

Pause.

SAMMY JR: No...no. I can hardly remember her, it's weird (*Pause.*) even her face is a blur...I remember my dad. He died seven days after my mum, seven days to the day. The sores on his skin started to bleed, his joints froze. I remember his groans, he spoke with his eyes in the end. He was a gentle man. He loved his kids, my mom. He never wanted to hurt anyone. He told me to look after my baby brothers and sisters, especially Bradley who isn't right in the head, he told me to do my duty…and be a man.

Pause.

MO: (*He looks different, calm, decisive.*) You asked me if I knew about the cave of course I knew. I masterminded the entire operation set up there. The chemical and biological weapons factory was my baby, so to speak. And we've plans, big plans. I admit it.

We have targeted the London underground for a gas attack in 2004, one of many planned operations. Of course, I can't say exactly when or where.

Anyway with or without me it's unstoppable. I admit it all.

I admit it all. So! What happens now?

And Hundreds and Thousands: Play 7

Lights up – a lurid orange, a dazzling scorching heat.

COOKIE and ANGELICA squat in the sand in the only bit of shade. COOKIE fans herself with an old, torn menu. They have dirty, bloody napkins tied around their mouths.

HARRY'S WIFE stands and watches.

In an old vegetable box a baby is crying. This is PARVANA.

From the back, HARRY appears.

He stops.

COOKIE and ANGELICA pull the napkins from their mouths.

ANGELICA: He's back

COOKIE: Harry's back!

> *Slowly, HARRY'S WIFE turns, they face each other. They are both ashen and trembling.*

HARRY'S WIFE: So

> *Pause.*

HARRY: So

HARRY'S WIFE: After all
this time

HARRY: I'm back

HARRY'S WIFE: You're back

> *She flings herself into his arms, ferociously laughing and crying, planting a million kisses.*

I love you
I love you
I love you

COOKIE: Save your spit
Here
in this egg cup
Dear God
the waste

*From down his trousers he pulls out a plastic water bottle,
full. They stop, in wonderment, he brandishes it.*

HARRY: The water's
back on

In houses now
they
turn the tap
and...

He makes watery noises.

Cheering and chatter.

HARRY'S WIFE: But is it safe?

Pause. HARRY shrugs.

Patti Stuckerman
drank the water
the army gave her

It made her
vomit shit

A week later
she was dead

COOKIE: That Patti!
Always
trying to draw
attention
to her
little self.

Of course it's safe,
what
are you saying?

They'd poison us?

It's safe

The baby cries.

ANGELICA: Parvana

HARRY'S WIFE gets a bundle of rags from the box. They crowd round.

COOKIE: Just wet
your finger mind

HARRY'S WIFE moistens the baby's lips again and again, the child cries until she passes it to ANGELICA; gradually the child stops crying.

HARRY'S WIFE: Thank you
Angelica

Silence. HARRY passes the water around, each takes a sip. He is close to collapse.

HARRY: (*Drinking.*)
To Dallas

HARRY'S WIFE: To my darling's
safe return

COOKIE: To, perhaps, getting back
in business

ANGELICA: (*A whisper.*)
To our child,
to keeping
her alive

HARRY: I got a ride back

HARRY'S WIFE: A ride?

HARRY: A truck
 full of farmers
 The army
 gave them gas;

 promised them
 work for food

COOKIE: I'm not
 hearing this

HARRY: The road's gone

 There're still
 buildings standing

 Some have
 windows,

 the lights
 go on and off

 and

 army vehicles
 come and go.

 Others
 are shells

 where
 the people squat.

 Some set
 up shops.

 I could
 have bought
 a pair
 of Reeboks,

no laces
half size
different,

but otherwise
perfect!
Perfect condition

COOKIE: How much?

HARRY: Most
of the Malls
are mined

In the cemetery
children dig up
the bones
to fashion
toothpicks
and combs

ANGELICA: Sssh

HARRY: They want
workers
to build roads –
towns,

They give
them guns

COOKIE: Crazy people

HARRY: And trucks
and

COOKIE: Dollars?

A whisper.

There'll be truckloads
of workers
passing by

HARRY'S WIFE: Hungry workers

COOKIE: No…
thousands
thousands of
hungry and
thirsty
workers

She whispers.

all wanting
strong coffee
and…

HARRY'S WIFE: A first light
fry up

HARRY: I …
I…
I got these

From out of his trousers he takes out a dozen assorted plastic sachets of ketchup, mustard, salt, pepper.

COOKIE: Great
Ronald McDonald
quakes
in his boots

A chime, as if from a door. A large figure looms forward in green military fatigues.

GOD-GENERAL: Service!

Lights dip, a record from the jukebox plays Texas Country and Western.

A table and chair have been improvised. The GENERAL sits in front of a tiny bird skeleton and the skin of a large potato. He has a napkin tucked into his shirt collar. The hired help all hover. ANGELICA, still with PARVANA, stares.

GOD-GENERAL: (*Tucking in greedily, animated.*)
    Hanging's best
    You mark my words

    A bullet's
    too good for them

    Gassing's unreliable

    Give me a cold beer
    for every gassed corpse
    that's sat up and begged!

    With the rope
    I can despatch
    three hundred a day.

HARRY: As many as that

GOD-GENERAL: And
    That's with breaks
    For fag, shit and…

    He looks at ANGELICA.

    shag

    He chuckles.

    Some don't
    have the stomach
    but
    I can take
    my tucker
    watching

    He roars with laughter.

    It's the paperwork
    that
    slows you down

COOKIE: We heard

electricity's back on
in Valentine

GOD-GENERAL: Oh, the chair's
more fun,
Ma'am

I agree
with you
there

And I miss
the squeal
and sizzle

COOKIE: The smell
of
roasting flesh…

GOD-GENERAL: But I'd
rather
grill me a
hog chop
than
fry me a
cloth head

Pause.

HARRY'S WIFE: So they
look
like us?

GOD-GENERAL: Naked
they're not
dissimilar

Their eyes
are
closer together

HARRY: Of course

GOD-GENERAL: Their necks
  thicker

HARRY'S WIFE: Their foreheads
  lower

COOKIE: There must
  be hundreds
  now

GOD-GENERAL: In the camps?
  Thousands

  COOKIE spoons a dollop of something onto his plate.

COOKIE: I am
  Cookie Pottleheimer

  The sole proprietress

  My husband's
  name
  was formally
  above the door

HARRY'S WIFE: Until his…

  They share a look.

  accident

COOKIE: May I introduce my hired help

  She gestures introductions.

  Harry – kitchen hand

  Harry's Wife – chief waitress

  Angelica – second waitress

HARRY: Are you alone sir?

  No answer. The GENERAL eats, he stares at ANGELICA, she stares back.

You have no driver?

No answer. The GENERAL eats.

It's a long trip
here
from anywhere
Flint
and the heat
makes the tyres
sweat and split

Does your vehicle
require
service perhaps?

Is there
a convoy
following?

GOD-GENERAL: I ask the questions, retard

*He stands, walks about. ANGELICA's eyes follow him,
everywhere.*

Something
puzzles me.
Last
couple of hundred
miles
all I passed
was piles
of bones
Yet you
good folks

He looks at ANGELICA, grins, and picks his teeth.

Look
plump and…
fresh and

juicy

COOKIE: (*Quickly.*)
    Careful husbandry
    Of our resources
    sir

    For

    We were
    a thriving
    little stop off
    once

HARRY'S WIFE: Good food

HARRY: Better than good

COOKIE: And service
    second to none

    Real teamwork
    selfless
    and seamless

HARRY: We could perhaps provide
    a valuable
    service for you, sir

HARRY'S WIFE: For you and yours

COOKIE: This road building
    project

HARRY: Army sponsored

HARRY'S WIFE: As we understand

HARRY: Will bring
    hungry workers
    to our door

HARRY'S WIFE: And hungry troops
    we're sure

COOKIE: We have the skills
    culinary wise
    and just
    a little digging
    will recover
    pots and pans
    and…

HARRY'S WIFE: Knives, spoons
    and forks

HARRY: Personally
    I find meat
    cooked
    over the bare blue flame

HARRY'S WIFE: In the spare wholesome
    air

HARRY: Under the shimmer of stars p'raps

HARRY'S WIFE: Or God's glorious sunshine

COOKIE: Tastier,
    but…

GOD-GENERAL: There's a but…

HARRY'S WIFE: We need provisions

COOKIE: We need…
    investment

HARRY: We have
    a spill
    of store food

    Only a spill

COOKIE: A little flour
    that's all

HARRY: We can start simply
    With your help –

eggs
bacon –

bread

COOKIE: Or failing that –
Dollars, sir
will do
that'll do nicely, sir
to take
to market…
somewhere
It's rumoured

You can pick
up
a tin of beans
in Dallas

HARRY: Miraculous

COOKIE: Baked beans
and chipolatas

and pickled gherkins
in barrels
in Fort Worth

Houston's still
a no-entry zone
we know

but

Austin
flew out
pepper sauce
and hot chilli dogs

GENERAL laughs.

GOD-GENERAL: I love it

I love you
little folks

Your spunk
Your grit
Your guts

Tillin' the dusty earth

Lassoing the wild boar

Taking the chickens'
speckled eggs

to sell

at roadsides

stirs something
deep

inside

Pause. He ogles ANGELICA.

To ANGELICA.

What you eyeballin'?

ANGELICA freezes. They all do.

Why
you been lookin' at me
like
I'm shit
on your shoe?

Since I
stepped
in the light

Mm?

Why?

Fucking 'ho'…

COOKIE: (*Sternly.*)
    General
    I must protest
    you see
    the sign
    above
    the door

Looking about helplessly.

    Profanity's
    forbidden
    here!

GOD-GENERAL: (*To ANGELICA.*)
    This good lady
    this fine
    good lady
    this decent lady
    pays you
    to put out
    squaw

    And

    You looking at me
    like I'm shit on your shoe?

Silence.

    Wiggling
    your
    skinny butt

    Wobblin'
    Your saggy
    tits

    You looking at me
    bitch

    like I'm

shit, shit, shit

on your shoe

He takes a tin cup, hurls it at her, it hits her, he stands.

COOKIE: Enough!
You're barred

How dare you sir
Angelica
is a valued
employee
here…

He grabs COOKIE, forces her to her knees viscously, and puts a gun to her head.

(*Whispering quickly.*)
But
General, sir
what about
dessert?

Pause.

GOD-GENERAL: (*Greedily.*)
Dessert?

COOKIE: Of course,
dessert!

GOD-GENERAL: Dessert!

COOKIE: Hot brownies

HARRY: Nutty

HARRY'S WIFE: And chewy

GOD-GENERAL: Dessert!

COOKIE: Trifle

HARRY: Sparkly sponge fingers

HARRY'S WIFE: Soaking
in a fiery rum

COOKIE: Cheesecake
glazed and

ANGELICA: (*She is seductive, caressing.*)
Quivering

From behind, she kisses his ears, his head, his neck. He lets the gun drop.

COOKIE: Garnished
with a single
strawberry

HARRY: Succulent fruits

HARRY'S WIFE: The downy peach
Glossy green apples

HARRY: Blueberries
that smell
of sky

They encircle him. HARRY leads him back to his seat. HARRY'S WIFE pulls out the chair. ANGELICA tucks in a napkin.

COOKIE: Steam baked
in
a flaky pastry pie

HARRY: Melt in your mouth

HARRY'S WIFE: And served
on the side

COOKIE: drizzled
with hot
toffee
sauce

HARRY'S WIFE: sprinkled

HARRY: with cheeky
    chopped
    pistachio

COOKIE: and in a
    creamy
    dollop

HARRY: topped

HARRY'S WIFE: with a
    cheery sprig
    of fresh
    garden
    mint

ANGELICA: Ice cream!!!

In one sudden movement they restrain him while ANGELICA slits his throat. Long silence. Then they whisper.

COOKIE: That was perfect
    just like the old days
    as I remember
    as I remember

    Perfect timing

HARRY: I give
    the trucks
    two days

HARRY'S WIFE: Less

COOKIE: I have
    so many
    plans

    She looks around.

tables
and…

HARRY: (*Helpfully.*)
chairs

COOKIE: Yes,
knives
forks
and spoons

HARRY'S WIFE: Napkins
in stone rings

HARRY: Like
ancient
scrolls

COOKIE: Candles!

ANGELICA: And flowers?

HARRY: Daisies

COOKIE: Blue bonnets

HARRY'S WIFE: Wild orchids

COOKIE: Mm!
Too
pricey

They all look at her.

No
perhaps,
you're right
anyway
a discerning clientele
will expect
the cover charge
to reflect…

an ambitious
ambience

Light the fire
Angelica

ANGELICA: It's lit

HARRY: You'll need
a hand
with jointing

HARRY'S WIFE: We'll all help

COOKIE: Quick
Angelica
a bowl
for the blood

Gravy makes
a roast dish

Juke box: 'Catch a Falling Star', very soft as an underscore.

Lights down. With the great knife a slice is cut. It is just about to be served to the audience – then blackout.

WWW.OBERONBOOKS.COM

www.ingramcontent.com/pod-product-compliance
Ingram Content Group UK Ltd.
Pitfield, Milton Keynes, MK11 3LW, UK
UKHW031252020325
455690UK00007B/90